WILMA
RUDOLPH

by
Wayne Coffey

BLACKBIRCH PRESS, INC.

Woodbridge, Connecticut

Published by Blackbirch Press, Inc.
260 Amity Road
Woodbridge, CT 06525

©1993 Blackbirch Press, Inc.
First Edition

Printed in Hong Kong
10 9 8 7 6 5 4 3 2

Editor: Bruce Glassman
Photo Research: Grace How
Illustrations: David Taylor

Library of Congress Cataloging-in-Publication Data

Coffey, Wayne R.
　　Wilma Rudolph / Wayne Coffey. — 1st ed.
　　　　p.　　cm. — (Olympic gold)
　　Includes bibliographical references and index.
　　Summary: This Olympic star overcame extraordinary adversity, including crippling polio, to become the fastest woman in the world by 1960.
　　ISBN 1-56711-004-5
　　1.Rudolph, Wilma, 1940-　　—Juvenile Literature.
2. Runners (Sports)—United States—Biography—Juvenile literature. [1. Rudolph, Wilma, 1940-　. 2. Track and field athletes. 3. Afro-Americans—Biography.] I. Title.
II. Series.
GV1061.15.R83C64　1993
796.42 '092—dc20　　　　　　　　　　　　　　　92-41292
[B]　　　　　　　　　　　　　　　　　　　　　　　　　CIP
　　　　　　　　　　　　　　　　　　　　　　　　　　　AC

Contents

Courage and Determination

"I was mad, and I was going to beat these illnesses, no matter what."

When the young Wilma Rudolph attended Burt High School in Clarksville, Tennessee, she was a basketball star known all over the state. From the Great Smoky Mountains in the east to the city of Memphis in the west, the tall, spindly girl had few equals. At age 15, she was an all-state player, scoring 803 points in just 25 games. Almost nobody could stop her quick, darting moves and explosive drives to the basket.

Opposite:
Although she was constantly sick and nearly crippled as a child, Wilma Rudolph grew up to be the fastest woman in the world.

She Could Run

Wilma's greatest asset, without a doubt, was the way she could run. Whenever there was a loose ball, Wilma seemed to get there first. If she had the ball on a fast break, she made defenders look like statues as she bolted right past them.

Nobody was more impressed with Wilma than a man named Ed Temple. A widely respected track-and-field coach at Tennessee State University, he also worked as a basketball referee. As a guest referee, he could scout out promising young athletes all over the world. One night, Temple was officiating at a high school basketball game where the Burt High School girls' team was playing. One player who kept drawing his attention was Wilma Rudolph. Temple just imagined what her strides could achieve on a track field.

Soon enough, Ed Temple would have the answer to his question. He played a pivotal role in Wilma's development—first on his Tennessee State track team, then on a national level, and finally in the Olympics. It was at the Olympics in Rome, in 1960, that Wilma Rudolph emerged as one of the greatest stars in the history of the Olympic Games.

Wilma's performance and her easygoing manner made her a huge favorite with sports fans. In France, they called her "La Perle Noire" (The Black Pearl). In Italy, she was called "La Gazella Nera" (The Black

Gazelle). Photographs and stories about her appeared in newspapers and magazines all over the globe.

Illness and Courage

Wilma's real triumph began long before she had ever heard of Rome, the Olympics, or track and field. When she was only four years old, crippling illnesses had plagued her frail body. She had lost the use of her left leg. For several years, she had not even been able to walk. A big outing for Wilma had been when her mother wrapped her up, boarded a bus, and took her to a medical clinic in Nashville, about 45 miles away from her hometown of Clarksville. Doctors had doubted that she would ever have full use of her legs.

There were times when Wilma had felt like giving in to her illnesses. But she found the strength to keep fighting.

There had been times when Wilma had felt like giving up, and giving in to her illnesses. But she had found the strength to keep fighting. In her autobiography, *Wilma*, she wrote:

I went through the stage of asking myself, "Wilma, what is this existence all about? Is it all about being sick all the time? It can't be." So I started getting angry about things, fighting back in a new way, with a vengeance. I think I started acquiring a competitive

7

spirit right then and there, a spirit that would make me successful in sports later on. I was mad, and I was going to beat these illnesses, no matter what. No more taking what comes, no more drifting off, no more wondering. Enough was enough.

A "Miracle"

That same little girl became the fastest female runner in the world, winning three gold medals in track and field at the 1960 Olympics. Considering where she came from, it was almost a miracle. "It was the greatest experience of my life, especially after my childhood problems," Wilma said.

Not long after, she became only the third woman to be named winner of the prestigious Sullivan Award. The award honors the best amateur athlete in the United States. Wilma and her parents were special

Wilma grew up and became the fastest female runner in the world, winning three gold medals at the 1960 Olympics. Considering where she came from, it was almost a miracle.

guests of President John F. Kennedy at the White House. Wilma made numerous speeches and appearances around the country. After she wrote her autobiography, it was made into a television movie. In the early 1980s, she even formed her own foundation in an effort to help aspiring athletes.

2

A Hard Beginning

*"We didn't have too much money
back then. But we had everything
else, especially love."*

Wilma Rudolph was born on June 23, 1940, in the town of St. Bethlehem, Tennessee. She was the twentieth of 22 children of Blanche and Ed Rudolph, and she almost didn't survive her own birth. Born two months prematurely, Wilma weighed just four and a half pounds. She was so small and so weak that her life was in almost constant danger. It didn't help that in the poverty-stricken areas, where most black families lived in segregation, both doctors and medical facilities were in great demand and short supply, especially for blacks.

Hard Work and Poverty

Ed Rudolph worked as a porter for the railroad. His wife was employed as a domestic, helping people with household chores. The town was a small farming community where folks grew corn and tobacco. Making ends meet wasn't easy—especially when Wilma's parents had so many young mouths to feed. Shortly after Wilma was born, the Rudolphs moved to Clarksville, a bigger town, where there were more job opportunities.

Even with both of them working hard, the Rudolphs earned little money and had to endure poor living conditions. The family was crammed into a small rented cottage. There was no electricity. The bathroom was an outhouse in the back-yard. Wilma's mother made clothes for her children out of discarded flour sacks. The Rudolphs could have applied to get welfare from the federal government to ease their hardship, but they wanted no part of it. They were proud people. They wanted no handouts.

Living with Racism

Most of the white people in Clarksville lived in comfortable, well-kept houses. Many whites worked at the big tire factory in town, where black people were denied jobs for years. When they were finally allowed to work there, they were given the most menial (low-paying) jobs. Wilma saw white people living well and driving fancy cars. Even as a little girl she knew that it wasn't right that African Americans could not enjoy the same privileges. Wilma made up her mind that she would do everything in her power not to let people hold her back just because of the color of her skin.

Wilma made up her mind that she would not let people hold her back just because of the color of her skin.

Despite substandard living conditions, the Rudolph family managed to get by. "We didn't have too much money back then," Wilma wrote in her autobiography. "But we had everything else, especially love."

Still, it was difficult for Wilma to feel like a normal kid. She was sick so often that she didn't even go to school until second grade. At different times, she suffered from whooping cough, double pneumonia, and scarlet fever. Even when she got a simple cold, it often lasted for weeks because she didn't have the strength to fight it off.

Crippled by Polio

Wilma's greatest burden was polio, which struck her at a very young age and left her with a crooked left foot and leg. For years, Wilma had practically no use of her left leg.

When she tried to play with other children, her limp sometimes made her the subject of cruel taunts. A few mean kids would call her a "cripple" and laugh at her handicap. As the condition worsened, Wilma couldn't play at all. She was confined to bed or a chair.

At age five, Wilma began wearing a heavy steel brace to straighten her leg. It started above her knee and went all the way down to the special shoes she was forced to wear. The shoes were brown and clunky, and Wilma hated them, even if they were necessary to help her get better. She wore the brace and shoes for six years.

Young Wilma spent much of her early childhood in bed recovering from such illnesses as whooping cough, double pneumonia, scarlet fever, and polio. Often, she was so exhausted that it would take her weeks to recover from a simple cold.

The brace wasn't only unattractive and heavy, but it was also a constant reminder to young Wilma that she was different from other kids. Saddened and frustrated as she was by her situation, the young girl showed a remarkable positive attitude. Instead of complaining or feeling sorry for herself, she focused on doing everything possible to get better. Wilma's mother used to marvel at the quiet courage and unusual determination of her little girl.

A Slow Recovery

There were serious doubts about whether Wilma would ever have full use of her leg. She had been undergoing treatments on it for years.

When it was clear Wilma needed more intensive medical attention, her mother started taking her to a Nashville clinic. The trips took up the whole day. Wilma would undergo four hours of treatment as doctors tested her leg by twisting it and lifting it. They had Wilma exercise it. They gave her massages and whirlpool baths, seeking the best therapy to stimulate her leg to get it stronger. Later, at home, Wilma's mother, and sometimes her brothers and sisters, took turns massaging the ailing leg. Everyone in the family wanted to help Wilma in any way they could.

Opposite:
Wilma had an important break-through at age 10. It was then, at a Sunday morning church service, that she took a walk in public without her brace.

Wilma knew that her disability was hard for the whole family. To keep her spirits up, Wilma taught herself to walk without a limp. Because of the weakness of her bad leg, it was natural for her to favor the stronger one. With discipline and practice, however, she perfected a regular walk. The little girl figured that her mother would be encouraged that she was walking so well, though the recovery was long and slow.

Walking on Her Own Again

Nothing helped Wilma's spirits more than what she did one Sunday morning shortly before she turned 10. The Rudolphs went to church, as they always had, except this time Wilma left her dreaded leg brace at home. Since she had begun wearing the brace, she had never gone out in public without it. But she had worked hard to teach herself to walk without the brace, and without a limp. As Wilma walked down the aisle, she felt everyone's eyes upon her. She heard people whispering: "Look at Wilma, she's walking without the brace." People streamed over to tell her how happy they were for her and to express their faith that she would continue to get better. A giant smile was fixed on Wilma's face. She said later it was one of the most important moments of her life.

Wilma wasn't finished with the brace for good though. She wore it constantly until she was 10. Then she wore it on and off until she was 12, whenever her leg ached or felt uncomfortable.

When Wilma was about to finish sixth grade, doctors decided that the years of therapy had paid off. Wilma did not need the brace at all any longer. Her mother packed it up and shipped it off to Nashville.

Young Wilma felt free for the first time in her life. Finally, she felt totally healthy and able-bodied. There wouldn't be any more looks of pity from strangers or teasing from other kids. In a number of ways, Wilma Rudolph felt as if her life were starting anew. She could hardly wait. She would be a seventh grader in the fall, which meant she would go to Burt High School. And now she had the wonderful gift of being able to go out to play.

Wilma Discovers Basketball

That summer, Wilma saw some kids playing basketball in a little downtown park. It looked like so much fun. Wilma was eager to start playing, too. Sometimes the kids played at one of the town parks. Other times, she would join with other kids in somebody's backyard, where there was a peach basket nailed to a tree. Because

neither Wilma nor the rest of the kids could afford a real basketball, they used whatever they had—a rubber ball, or even a big beach ball. It didn't matter, Wilma just loved playing the game. Because her legs still weren't that strong, she couldn't run around as much as the others.

As soon as Wilma could walk without her brace, she eagerly became active in all kinds of sports. One of her favorites was basketball. She played with neighborhood kids who used a peach basket for a hoop.

The Joy of Sports

Blanche Rudolph was very protective of her little girl. She was afraid that even a minor injury might ruin all those years of painstaking therapy. "Now, you take it easy," Mrs. Rudolph would say before leaving for work. And then Wilma would run off to play basketball. One day, after returning home, Wilma's mother asked her daughter what she had done that day.

"I played basketball all afternoon," Wilma replied.

Mrs. Rudolph gave her daughter a good, sound scolding, warning her about the danger of straining herself. Wilma understood her mother was just trying to protect her, but being able to play basketball with other kids was probably the greatest pleasure she'd ever experienced. How could she not play?

Joining the School Team

Wilma's older sister, Yvonne, played on the school basketball team. When basketball season arrived, Wilma wanted to play, too. The school had just one team for grades 7 through 12. Even though Wilma was young and inexperienced, the coach, Clinton Gray, put her on the team.

Wilma never got to play in a game her first season, but she had fun anyway. She enjoyed traveling around to the different schools her team played against, and she enjoyed studying the strategies and movements of the players on the basketball court. For Wilma, it was great just being part of a team. And even if she didn't know it then, she was on her way to becoming an important star.

3

A High School Basketball Star

Wilma reminded Coach Gray of a mosquito, the way she buzzed about. And from that day on, Wilma Rudolph had a new nickname: "Skeeter."

n the 1950s, when Wilma was growing up, not many girls were serious about sports. One reason for this was that, at the time, some people had the attitude that girls who were athletes were not feminine. These people believed that only boys were supposed to compete in sports and be physically strong.

Loving to Win

Young Wilma didn't care for this attitude one bit. It seemed ridiculous to her that someone might think her less of a girl because of her interest in competitive sports. She loved to play, and she loved to win. Why should she be denied fun just because she happened to be a girl?

19

Ready to Play

Wilma's basketball career took off in her sophomore year at Burt High. She had spent three full seasons on Coach Gray's bench, and the idleness was frustrating.

Clinton Gray was a demanding coach. He wouldn't let any of his girls play if they didn't have at least a B average. He pushed them hard in practice. He frequently yelled at the players during time-out. This was one habit of Coach Gray's that Wilma couldn't stand. Wilma had her differences with the coach. There were a couple of times when Wilma got so angry that she actually quit the team. But she was always back at practice the next day.

"Skeeter" in Action

Wilma wasn't merely a starter by the time she entered tenth grade. She had been watching and practicing for three years, and she was quick, which gave her a big advantage. Her long arms also made her a terror on defense. One of her trademarks was stealing the ball from opponents as they dribbled. Out of nowhere, Wilma would strip the ball away and race ahead for a lay-up. Wilma was all over the court in just about every game she played, and during practice, too. One day she was sprinting after the ball, her spindly arms and legs churning, and she wound up sprawled out on the floor, not far from where Coach Gray was standing. Wilma reminded him of a mosquito, the way she buzzed about. From that day on, Wilma had a new nickname: "Skeeter."

Triumph on the Courts

One of Wilma's most memorable games was in a tournament right on the Burt High team's home court. That day, Wilma led Burt High to victory by scoring 32 points— and not missing a single shot during the entire game. The crowd roared its approval for Wilma, who got the biggest ovation of any player. The next day in school, classmates and friends heartily congratulated her. All the compliments made Wilma feel very special. For the first time, she felt that she was a somebody at Burt High School.

For the first time, Wilma felt that she was somebody at Burt High School.

The Burt High girls' basketball team won a conference title that season. For Wilma, this first real season on the court was just the beginning of her basketball triumphs. The following year was even better. Burt High School had one of the finest girls' basketball teams in Tennessee history. Wilma averaged 35 points per game, and with her defensive skills, gave opposing teams a lot of trouble. Teammate Nancy

Bowen, a close friend of Wilma's, had a superb year, too, scoring 38 points per game. With Wilma and Nancy on its side, the Burt High girls' team proved unbeatable. In a close and tough game, the Burt High girls defeated Merry High School of Jackson, Tennessee, to capture the state championship.

Wilma on the Tracks

Basketball wasn't Wilma's only love at this point. More and more, she realized how much she enjoyed running. In the spring, Clinton Gray put away the basketballs until the next season and became coach of Burt High School's track team. In the first two years that Wilma was on the team, she didn't lose a single race. She competed mostly in sprints—the 100-yard dash and the 200-yard dash. Wilma didn't know much about proper running techniques, but it hardly mattered. Rarely did anybody finish even close to her.

About this time, Ed Temple, who was the coach of Tennessee State University, began watching Wilma's performance closely. Ed Temple did not have any doubts that this long-limbed girl from Clarksville, Tennessee, had enormous promise. How far could she go? It was difficult to say, but the coach was eager to find out.

4

Training for the Gold

"You've got four years to get there yourself, but you've got to work hard . . . and pay the price."

In the spring of 1956, Ed Temple visited the Rudolph home in Clarksville. Each summer, he conducted a running program at Tennessee State for the best high school athletes. He wanted Wilma to be part of the program. All of her expenses would be taken care of. Wilma would be closely supervised and would have to abide by strict rules—as all of Ed Temple's running students did. Ed and Blanche Rudolph had questions at first. But they became convinced that Temple was a trustworthy man, apart from being a splendid coach. Under Temple's direction, women's track and field at Tennessee State had achieved national rank. When Coach Temple told Wilma's parents that their daughter had a good chance of getting a college scholarship because of her running skill, they agreed to let Wilma take part in the program.

A Great Coach

Under Ed Temple's guidance, Wilma progressed rapidly. She was learning so much that it was like being in a classroom. She found out about proper breathing techniques, staying relaxed, and other methods that made her running smoother and faster. Wilma was one of a squad of talented young runners. One event that quickly became Wilma's favorite was the 440-yard relay, in which four girls teamed up, each one running 110 yards. Still running full speed as she finished her stretch of the distance, each girl would place a small baton in the hand of the next runner. Wilma especially loved the teamwork of the relay event.

After weeks of hard training, Ed Temple's team traveled north to Philadelphia for a prestigious national competition called the Amateur Athletic Union championships. Wilma had never been in the North before, nor had she ever stayed in a big-city hotel. Wilma felt overwhelmed by the size of everything. The downtown buildings were so tall. The stadium where the meet was held, Franklin Field, was the most massive place Wilma had ever seen.

The First National Race

The Tennessee girls may have been awed. But, judging by their performances, no one ever would have known it. Competing in the junior division, the girls dominated the meet. Wilma said later it was one of the most exhausting days of her life. Coach Temple entered Wilma in three events: the 75-yard dash, the 100-yard dash, and the 440-yard relay. Because there were so many runners from all over the country, each event had two qualifying races to determine who would advance to the final race. Wilma won both of her qualifying races in the 75-yard dash and then raced to an easy triumph in the final. She also won both qualifiers in the 100 and again captured the victory in the final. The relay team also triumphed. When the day was over, Wilma had competed in nine separate races—and had won all nine.

Ed Temple was delighted with Wilma's performance in Philadelphia, but it wasn't his style to gush about such things. "You're coming along real well, Wilma," the coach said to the day's biggest star.

Shortly after returning to Tennessee from Philadelphia, Coach Temple talked to Wilma

25

for the first time about the Olympic Games. Wilma had only a vague idea of what the Olympics were about. International sports weren't something too many poor kids from Tennessee thought about. Besides, Wilma wasn't even a junior in high school yet. It was hard for her to imagine being in an event where she would run against the greatest athletes in the world. But Ed Temple was convinced that Wilma deserved a chance to try to make the Olympic team, no matter how young she was.

Olympic Trials in Seattle

The tryouts, or trials, for the U.S. Olympic team were held in Seattle, Washington, in 1956. Temple sent several of his best college runners from Tennessee State. He also sent Wilma. The most famous member of the Tennessee State team was Mae Faggs. Faggs had already set numerous U.S. track-and-field records and had won medals in the 1952 Olympics. Mae Faggs was from Harlem in New York City. She and Wilma became close friends.

A Special Friendship

Mae Faggs and Wilma Rudolph were an odd pair to see together. Mae was a tiny 4 feet 10 inches. Wilma, who was five years younger, was nearly 6 feet tall. When they

At Tennessee State University, Wilma became a close friend of Mae Faggs, another track-and-field star. The two friends offered encouragement and support to each other and often competed in track-and-field events together.

ran together, it seemed as if Mae's short, powerful legs had to take three strides to cover the same ground Wilma covered with one stride. Mae urged Wilma not to worry about what other people thought of her. "You owe it to yourself to do your best every time you race," Mae would tell her.

Before races, Wilma would get so wound up that she would feel sick to her stomach.

The queasy feeling stayed with her through-out her running career. As the Olympic trials approached, Wilma felt worse than ever before. She was getting more and more nervous. Here she was, a high school kid, up against the greatest female athletes in America. Wilma felt very scared. Mae was always there to comfort her. "Skeeter, baby," Mae said to Wilma, "you just stick with me, and everything's going to be all right."

In Seattle, Coach Temple entered Wilma and Mae Faggs in the 200-meter sprint. Wilma did exactly as Mae suggested. In fact, Wilma stayed so close to Mae in the 200-meter sprint that the two runners crossed the finish line at exactly the same moment to share first place. At age 16, Wilma was going to Melbourne, Australia. She was going to be in the 1956 Olympics! "I told you to stick with me. I didn't tell you to beat me," Mae said with a smile.

The 1956 Olympics

Wilma couldn't stop thinking about where she was heading. It was like a fairy tale to her. Back home in Clarksville, people were just as excited. Knowing that the Rudolphs didn't have much money to spare, people took up a collection to buy Wilma some things for her big trip. It was a loving gesture that Wilma has never forgotten. When she needed it most, the people in her hometown rallied around her.

There was a two-week training camp in Los Angeles prior to the Olympics. Wilma took the first airplane ride of her life to get there. It was all so new to her that when the flight attendant offered her a meal, Wilma declined. She thought she would have to pay extra for the food until Mae explained that there was no charge.

One Race Short of the Finals

After a stop in Hawaii, the exhausting two-day trip ended when the plane touched down in Australia. Wilma's first race was a qualifying competition in the 200 meters. The first three finishers would advance to a second qualifying round. As Wilma crouched into the starting blocks, her mind was totally focused. She didn't know whom she was running against. She was thinking solely of covering those 200 meters as fast as she could.

And 16-year-old Wilma, the youngest member of the entire U.S. Olympic team, did exactly that. She raced to a third-place finish. She had beaten all but two of the women in the field, all of whom were much more experienced. The next challenge was the semifinal race. This time, only the top two women would advance to the Olympic finals.

Against even stiffer competition in the semifinals, Wilma again placed third. But this time, coming in third was not good enough. Wilma had failed to qualify for the finals, and she felt awful about it. At that moment, she couldn't accept that it was a great accomplishment just to be competing in the Olympics. She felt that she had let herself down—indeed, that she had let all of America down. She could barely sleep. She cared even less about eating than before. Teammates came by her room to console her, but Wilma had a hard time even listening. She was miserable.

Refusing to Quit

Wilma's defeat did teach her an important lesson. It taught her the danger of being overconfident. It made her realize that she couldn't just step to the starting line and win every race handily. If she was going to keep improving, she had to rely on more than her remarkable natural ability.

The true champions, Wilma learned, are those who try even harder after a defeat.

It turned out to be one of the most important lessons of Wilma's life. She realized that truly successful people are the ones who learn how to lose. Nobody wins all the time. True champions, Wilma learned, try even harder after a defeat. It was an important lesson that Wilma never forgot.

Triumph in the Relay

Wilma overcame her disappointment about not making the Olympic finals in the 200 meters. She turned her attention to the other event in which she was competing, the 440-yard relay.

Besides Wilma, the American relay team consisted of Mae Faggs, Margaret Matthews, and Isabelle Daniels. Few expected the U.S. foursome to be among the top finishers. There were too many other strong teams. Mae ran the first leg of the relay, turning in a great effort that put her right up with the leaders. After Margaret finished her 110-yard sprint, she handed the baton to Wilma, who was able to outsprint a couple of competitors. Isabelle, running the last, or anchor, leg of the race, sped toward the finish, crossing the line just behind the powerful teams from Australia and the Soviet Union. The U.S. team had surprised everybody by finishing third. Wilma had won a bronze medal.

A Hero's Homecoming

Wilma received a hero's welcome when she returned home to Clarksville. At Burt

When Wilma returned home from her first Olympics in Melbourne, Australia, a special assembly was held in her honor at Burt High School. Along with a standing ovation, Wilma received a big bouquet of flowers and praise from all her teachers and peers.

High, there was a special assembly to honor her. Wilma received a standing ovation and a big bouquet of flowers. The principal gave a speech about how proud everyone was of her and then called upon Wilma to make a speech. Wilma thanked her schoolmates and the people in the community for all their encouragement.

Although she was only starting her junior year in high school, her taste of victory in Australia made Wilma burn with a new determination. Wilma made a promise to herself. "You've got four years to get there yourself," she said. "But you've got to work hard for those four years and pay the price."

1960

ROME, ITALY

EARLY DAYS

Wilma suffered through a physically and emotionally painful childhood. In her earliest years, she was stricken with whooping cough, double pneumonia, scarlet fever, and polio. Her bout with polio caused her left leg to become crooked; Wilma's doctors were not sure she would ever be able to walk normally again. Determined not to let her illness ruin her life, Wilma worked hard to walk without a brace and to regain the full use of her left leg. By the time she was 10, she took her first walk without her brace. Then, when she was in sixth grade, Wilma was able to put the brace away forever. As soon as the brace was gone, Wilma dove head-long into playing sports and having fun with her friends. *Top*: Wilma, age six, poses with her older sister, Yvonne. *Bottom*: By the time Wilma graduated from high school, she was recognized as one of America's most promising track-and-field athletes. Here, she and her friend, Mae Faggs, qualify for the 1956 women's Olympic track team in Washington, D.C. *Opposite*: From her earliest days at Tennessee State University, Wilma was one of the school's top track-and-field stars.

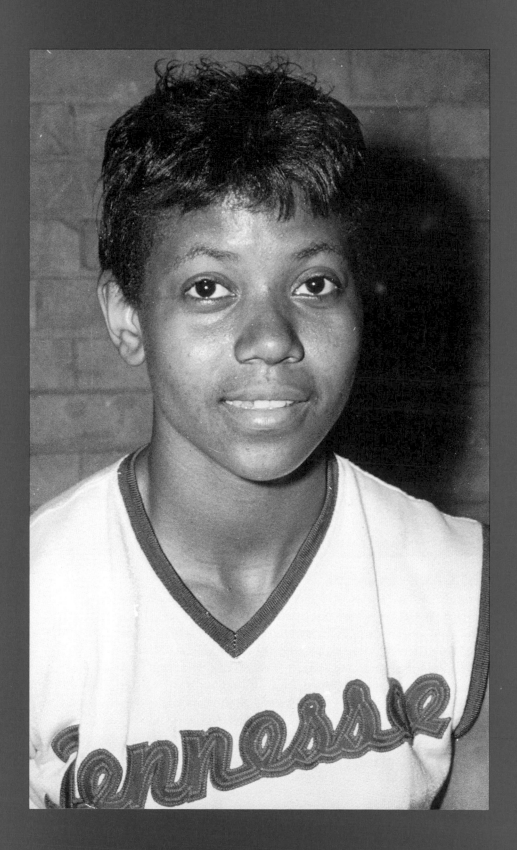

THE GAMES IN ROME

Although Wilma competed at the age of 16 in the 1956 Olympics in Melbourne, Australia, she did not advance past the second qualifying round. Disappointed and miserable, Wilma vowed that the next Olympics would be different. Four years later, in Rome, Italy, Wilma was ready to compete in three events. *Above*: The Olympic Stadium in Rome was packed with spectators as the opening ceremonies proceeded. *Opposite*: Wilma's first event at the 1960 Games was the 100-meter race, which she won easily.

THE FIRST GOLD

By the time Wilma competed in the 100-meter final, she had become one of the most popular athletes at the Rome Games. Wilma won the event with an unofficial world record of 11.0 seconds, breezing to the finish line well ahead of the other runners. Here, Wilma is awarded her first gold medal as second-place finisher, Dorothy Hyman of Great Britain, and third-place finisher, Giuseppina Leone of Italy, look on.

THE NEXT CHALLENGE

The 200-meter race was Wilma's strongest event. After breaking an Olympic record in the first qualifying heat, Wilma went on to win the gold with a final time of 24.0 seconds. *Below*: Wilma comes off the starting blocks in the 200-meter race. Because of her height and her extra-long legs, Wilma's starts were always slower than those of her competitors. *Opposite, top*: Wilma breaks the tape for a gold-medal victory in the 200-meter dash, where she finished a full four tenths of a second faster than the second-place runner. *Opposite, bottom*: Wilma savors her second gold medal with 200-meter silver medalist, Jutta Heine of West Germany (*right*), and bronze medalist, Dorothy Hyman (*left*) of Great Britain.

DANCE OF THE TIGERBELLES

Wilma's last event at the 1960 Games was the 4 x 100-meter relay. Running the fourth leg of the race, Wilma's final sprint gave her team—known as the Tigerbelles—a world record of 44.5 seconds. *Opposite*: Holding the baton high, Wilma breaks the tape to win the 4 x 100-meter relay. *Above*: The Tigerbelles (*left to right*): Wilma Rudolph, Lucinda Williams, Barbara Jones, and Martha Hudson. *Right*: America's four gold-medal runners stand on the winner's platform for the 4 x 100-meter awards ceremony.

HOME AS A HERO

Wilma returned home to a hero's welcome in the United States. Parades were held in her honor in New York City, Chicago, Washington, D.C., Atlanta, and, of course, Nashville and Clarksville, Tennessee. Here, part of the the proud Rudolph family poses with Wilma during a homecoming celebration in Nashville: On the left is mother, Blanche, in the center is father, Ed, and on the right is younger sister, Charlene. *Inset*: Wilma signs autographs for some of the 5,000 admirers who attended a program to honor her and other Olympians in 1960.

MORE PRAISE AND ACCOMPLISHMENTS

Honors and awards continued to pour in for months after Wilma's triumphs in Rome. In 1960, Wilma was voted Woman Athlete of the Year by the Associated Press and, soon afterward, was given the prestigious Sullivan Award for having done the most "to advance good sportsmanship throughout the year." *Right*: Wilma receives the Woman-Athlete-of-the-Year trophy in 1960. *Below*: Wilma poses with her Sullivan Award in 1962. *Opposite*: In 1963, Wilma finished her degree at Tennessee State University, graduating with a bachelor of science degree in elementary education.

A NEW STAR LOOKS UP TO HER IDOL

Florence Griffith Joyner, who is regarded as one of the greatest female track-and-field athletes of all time, embraces Wilma at the 1988 Olympic Games in Seoul, South Korea. "Flojo" acknowledges that Wilma is one of her track-and-field idols.

5

Life Changes in Many Ways

Personal decisions and important choices filled Wilma's life before 1960.

I n 1957, Wilma's personal life got in the way of her blossoming track-and-field career. It was then that she found out that she was going to have a baby. Wilma and her longtime boyfriend, Robert Eldridge, had just started to become sexually involved. Being young, neither of them had much awareness of birth control or of the risks of sexual activity. It was a difficult time for Wilma. She cared deeply for Robert, but the timing was all wrong. What was having a baby going to mean for her college scholarship? Her track career? Her dream to go to the next Olympics in Rome, Italy?

Life Goes On

After some rocky times, things worked out. In 1958, Wilma gave birth to a healthy baby girl, whom she named Yolanda. After some initial unhappiness, Wilma's parents and coach were supportive of Wilma as a new mother.

Robert stood by Wilma and wanted to marry her right away. It was a very hard decision for Wilma, who wanted to be able to raise her baby and live with the young

In 1958, Wilma gave birth to her daughter, Yolanda. Although being a mother while continuing her track-and-field career was a difficult challenge, Wilma's strong determination helped her achieve her goals.

man she loved. But Wilma wasn't ready to throw away her track career. Marriage would have to wait.

The Olympic Trials

The Olympic trials in 1960 were held at Texas Christian University, in the city of Fort Worth. Wilma qualified in three events: the 100-meter dash, the 200-meter dash, and the relay. She was one of the biggest stars in the entire track-and-field trial competition, among both men and women. In the 200, she set a world-record time of 22.9 seconds.

Before the U.S. Olympic team left for the pre-Olympic training session in Kansas, Wilma learned that the coach of the U.S. track team was going to be Ed Temple. Now the 20-year-old speedster had one more thing to be overjoyed about. She would be trained by her old coach. Everything was coming together. Now it was time for the challenge: to bring home those gold medals Wilma had wanted so badly four years earlier.

Time for the Games

Wilma got a great feeling about Rome right away. The Italian people were thrilled to be hosting the Olympics and went out of their way to make everyone feel welcome.

Wilma had a chance to see some of the city's world-famous sites, such as the Vatican and the ruins of the ancient Colosseum. She even took a liking to the hot, humid weather. The temperature, on many days, exceeded 100 degrees Fahrenheit. For some athletes, it was uncomfortable, like sitting in a steam bath. To Wilma, it was ideal. It felt just like the summers of her youth, back in Clarksville, Tennessee.

An Accident in Rome

As the competition approached, Wilma was in a confident frame of mind. Her practices were going splendidly. Coach Temple was every bit the source of comfort Wilma had expected he would be. He kept telling her that if she ran her race, nobody in the field could beat her.

The temperature cracked 100 degrees again the day before Wilma's first race. It was a Wednesday. Coach Temple didn't want his runners to exert themselves too much, so the schedule called only for a light workout. Along with several teammates, Wilma elected to do a little running on a field, right behind the Olympic stadium. It was covered with a thick, lush lawn, and there were sprinklers going. The runners were running on the grass, right through the sprinklers.

Near the end of the workout, Wilma made a final pass through the sprinkler, but just as she passed through it, her foot landed in a hole that she hadn't seen. Wilma sprawled out on the grass. She heard a pop. Her ankle throbbed with pain.

Wilma's teammates rushed over. Tears were streaming down her cheeks. As she lay there, horrible thoughts raced through her mind. Was her Olympic dream over? Were all those years of sweat and training going to be ruined because she ran through a sprinkler? Wilma didn't know how severe the injury was, but her ankle hurt a great deal and was swelling rapidly.

A trainer arrived on the scene and immediately applied an ice pack. Wilma was carried back to her room. The trainer taped her ankle tightly and instructed Wilma to keep it elevated. That way, blood would not rush to the area and cause any further swelling. Too much swelling would make it all but impossible to run on.

Making the Finals

The next morning, Wilma got out of bed and put her foot with the injured ankle on the floor. Gradually, she put weight on it. Miraculously, it felt okay, and supported her. "Thank God," Wilma said. It seemed as if everything would be all right, after all.

53

By a stroke of good fortune, Wilma's event that day was the qualifying heat for the 100-meter dash. It's a straight-ahead race, with no curves, which places much more stress on the ankles. Wilma felt sure that running straight wouldn't present a big problem.

Wilma didn't only win each qualifying race, but in the last one she even set a world record, with a time of 11.0 seconds! The track officials, however, determined that Wilma was aided by a slight wind at her back, meaning that the record would not be officially recognized.

The 100-Meter Challenge

Finally, the long-awaited day of the actual race arrived. Already, Wilma had become one of the most popular athletes at the Olympic Games, and the crowd continually chanted her name.

When the gun sounded, Wilma quickly hit her stride. Her strong, graceful legs blazed over the track as the roar of the crowd became louder and louder. By the 50-meter mark, she had sprinted into the lead. By 70 meters, she was well ahead. An instant later, Wilma dashed across the finish line—nobody else was even close. Her time was 11.0, but again, the wind reading made it an unofficial world record. The

Opposite:
Just a day before the Olympic Games began in Rome, Italy, Wilma injured her ankle while running through a water sprinkler. Remarkably, she was able to run the next day, winning the 100-meter and the 200-meter contests easily.

55

important thing was that Wilma had accomplished her goal. She had won her first gold medal. She raised her arms in celebration and acknowledged the cheers of the crowd.

The 200-Meter Challenge

The next challenge was the 200-meter race, Wilma's strongest event. Even running on the curves, Wilma's ankle gave her no trouble. In her initial heat, Wilma had a winning time of 23.2 seconds—an Olympic record. She went into Tuesday's final brimming with confidence. "There's nobody alive who can beat you in the two hundred. Go get it," Wilma told herself.

"Go get it" was exactly what Wilma did. Once more, she started well, cruising into full speed. Her acceleration turned her into a blur as she ran ahead of the other runners. Wilma's fiercest competitor, Jutta Heine of West Germany, was a distant second. When Wilma flashed past the finish, the appreciative crowd gave her another roaring ovation.

There were a few days to rest before the 400-meter relay on Friday. The U.S. team was from Tennessee State, a team that everyone knew as the Tigerbelles. Its members were Martha Hudson, Barbara Jones, Lucinda Williams, and, running the all-important anchor leg, Wilma Rudolph.

The Tigerbelles' Relay

Martha Hudson and Barbara Jones both ran excellent legs, and the U.S. team took an early lead. Lucinda Williams also ran well. As she streaked toward the end of her leg, Wilma was coiled, her arm outstretched behind her, waiting to take the baton and take off.

But as Lucinda made the handoff, Wilma juggled the baton for an instant. Critical time was lost. Other teams surged ahead. Once Wilma got a firm hold on the baton,

Even though critical time was lost during a bobbled handoff of the baton in the 4 x 100-meter relay, Wilma sprinted to a win that gave the Tigerbelles a world-record time of 44.5 seconds.

Opposite:
When Wilma returned from Rome as the first American woman ever to win three gold medals, she was one of the world's most famous and most admired athletes. Parades and other ceremonies greeted her in New York, Chicago, Washington D.C., Atlanta, and Tennessee, as other awards and honors poured in from all over the world.

she knew she had to run one of the greatest anchor legs of her life.

After a few strides, Wilma rapidly began to gain ground. She kept up her valiant charge. As she turned toward the finish, she was in the lead, and by then the whole stadium was certain that nobody was going to catch her. Wilma's final sprint gave the Tigerbelles a world-record time of 44.5 seconds. The crowd was going absolutely wild. The Tigerbelles—and especially the last Tigerbelle—had turned in a brilliant performance.

Three Gold Medals

Wilma Rudolph was the first American woman in Olympic history to capture three gold medals. As she stood on the victory stand with her teammates, the sounds of "The Star-Spangled Banner" filled the massive stadium.

Wilma felt that she was living a fantasy. She had become an international celebrity. Before leaving Rome, she and her U.S. teammates got a chance to meet Pope John XXIII. Coach Temple had arranged a tour of Europe, and at every stop, Wilma was greeted like a queen. Fans mobbed her for her autograph. Journalists and photographers asked her questions and took her picture. One admirer was so swept away

her that he took the shoes right off her feet and scurried away. The outpouring of affection was nonstop.

The Winner Comes Home

Wilma's reception in the United States was no different. There were parades and honors in New York, Chicago, Washington, D.C., Atlanta, and a host of other cities. In 1960, the Associated Press named her Woman Athlete of the Year. She won the Sullivan Award, which is given to the person voted the best amateur athlete in the nation. She received enough other honors and trophies to fill a warehouse.

Wilma felt that she was living a fantasy. She had become an international celebrity. Fans mobbed her for her autograph. The outpouring of affection was nonstop.

The greatest celebration of all, though, was in Clarksville, Tennessee. Just about all of the town's 40,000 people showed up. It was also the first time there had ever been a racially integrated event in Clarksville. African Americans and white people lined up all along the main street, saluting the local hero.

The folks in Clarksville also realized how remarkable Wilma's achievement was. A child who couldn't even walk and who was laughed at for being a cripple, had become an Olympic champion and the greatest woman athlete in U.S. Olympic history.

Wilma's brothers and sisters were at the celebration. Her daughter, Yolanda, was also there, and her parents, Ed and Blanche, who wouldn't have missed the big event for anything.

A child who couldn't even walk and who was laughed at for being a cripple, had become an Olympic champion and the greatest woman athlete in U.S. Olympic history.

A Lasting Legacy

On November 12, 1994, at age 54, Wilma died at her home in Brentwood, Tennessee. She had lived a long and successful life—fulfilling her dreams beyond her wildest expectations.

Wilma's final years had been busy. She worked with the Rudolph Foundation for underprivileged children and was also a popular teacher, lecturer, and spokesperson.

Awards and praise poured in for Wilma, right up until she died. In 1993, President Bill Clinton presented her with one of America's first National Sports Awards. Then, in September 1994, Wilma was inducted into the National Women's Hall of Fame.

Even when Wilma was a sickly girl struggling to survive, her parents knew she had deep determination. Wilma proved it when she took her first step without a brace. She proved it through all those difficult years of treatment. And she proved it at the Rome Olympics, where Wilma Rudolph became the fastest woman in the world.

Glossary

anchor leg The final segment of distance in a relay race.

blocks Foot supports for a crouching runner right before the start of a race.

handoff The exchange of the baton between the runners in a relay race.

heat A preliminary qualifying race.

lay-up A shot in basketball that is made by a player running up to the basket before shooting.

meter The basic unit of length in the metric system; equals 39.37 inches, or 3.28 feet.

pneumonia A disease that causes the lungs to become inflamed and, at times, congested.

segregation When people of different races are not allowed to live and go to school together.

semifinals The competition before the final round of a championship.

squad A team or large group.

vengeance Great desire and will.

For Further Reading

Arnold, Caroline. *The Olympic Summer Games.* New York: Franklin Watts, 1991.

Duden, Jane. *The Olympics.* New York: Crestwood House, 1991.

Jarrett, William. *Timetables of Sports History: The Olympic Games.* New York: Facts On File, 1990.

Merrison, Tim. *Field Athletics.* New York: Crestwood House, 1991.

Sandelson, Robert. *Track Athletics.* New York: Crestwood House, 1991.

Tatlow, Peter. *The Olympics.* New York: Franklin Watts, 1988.

Index

Photo Credits

Cover: AP/Wide World Photos; cover detail: AP/Wide World Photos; back cover: AP/Wide World Photos; p. 4: AP/Wide World Photos; p. 33: AP/Wide World Photos; p. 34 (top and bottom): AP/Wide World Photos; p. 35: AP/Wide World Photos; p. 36: AP/Wide World Photos; p. 37: Courtesy United States Olympic Committee; pp. 38–39: AP/Wide World Photos; p. 40: AP/Wide World Photos; p. 41 (top): Courtesy United States Olympic Committee; p. 41 (bottom): AP/Wide World Photos; p. 42: AP/Wide World Photos; p. 43 (top and bottom): AP/Wide World Photos; pp. 44–45 (with inset): AP/Wide World Photos; p. 46 (top and bottom): AP/Wide World Photos; p. 47: AP/Wide World Photos; p. 48: AP/Wide World Photos.